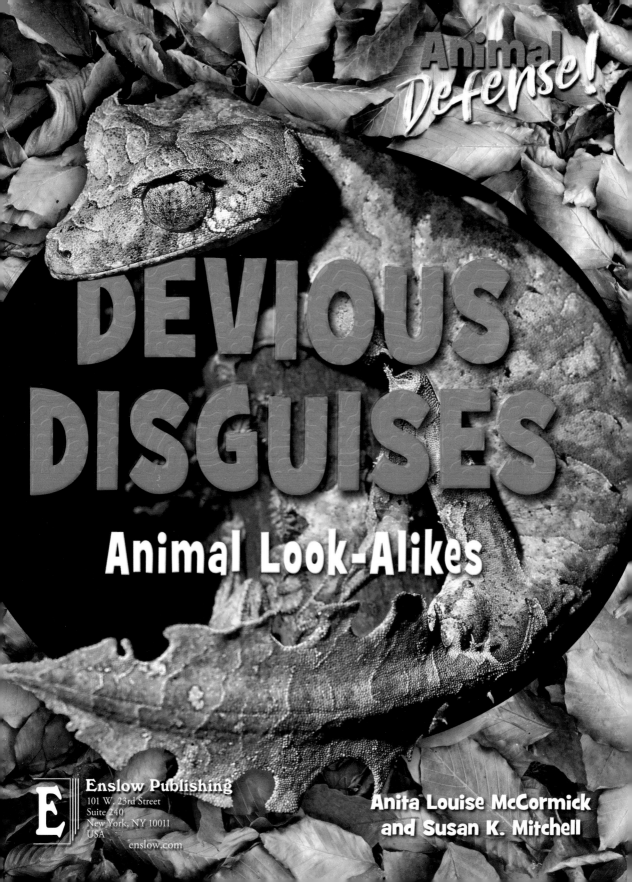

Animal
Defense!

DEVIOUS DISGUISES

Animal Look-Alikes

Enslow Publishing
101 W. 23rd Street
Suite 240
New York, NY 10011
USA

enslow.com

Anita Louise McCormick
and Susan K. Mitchell

These books are dedicated to Emily, who inspired the author.
—Susan K. Mitchell

Published in 2020 by Enslow Publishing, LLC.
101 W. 23rd Street, Suite 240, New York, NY 10011

Library of Congress Cataloging-in-Publication Data

Names: McCormick, Anita Louise, author. | Mitchell, Susan K., author.
Title: Devious disguises : animal look-alikes / Anita Louise McCormick and
    Susan K. Mitchell.
Description: New York : Enslow Publishing, 2020. | Series: Animal defense! |
    Audience: Grade 3-6. | Includes bibliographical references and index.
Identifiers: LCCN 2018048399| ISBN 9781978507166 (library bound) |
    ISBN 9781978508132 (paperback)
Subjects: LCSH: Mimicry (Biology)—Juvenile literature. | Animal defenses—
    Juvenile literature.
Classification: LCC QH546 .M34 2020 | DDC 581.4/7—dc23
LC record available at https://lccn.loc.gov/2018048399

Printed in the United States of America

To Our Readers: We have done our best to make sure all website addresses in this book were active and appropriate when we went to press. However, the author and the publisher have no control over and assume no liability for the material available on those websites or on any websites they may link to. Any comments or suggestions can be sent by email to customerservice@enslow.com.

Portions of this book originally appeared in *Animal Mimics: Look-alikes and Copycats*.

Photo Credits: Cover, p. 1 (Leaf-tailed Gecko) Ryan M. Bolton/Shutterstock.com; cover, p. 1 (leaves) ProKasia/Shutterstock.com; p. 6 Doug Perrine/Photolibrary/Getty Images; p. 10 Zety Akhzar/Shutterstock.com; p. 12 DJ Mattaar/Shutterstock.com; p. 15 (top and bottom) Matt Jeppson/Shutterstock.com; p. 19 Bildagentur Zoonar GmbH/Shutterstock.com; p. 21 (top) Kate Besler/Shutterstock.com; p. 21 (bottom) Paul Reeves Photography/Shutterstock.com; p. 25 Barbi Hofer/Shutterstock.com; p. 27 (top) Chris Rorabaugh/Shutterstock.com; p. 27 (bottom) Nashepard/Shutterstock.com; p. 31 (left and right) Dirk Ercken/Shutterstock.com; p. 35 (top) Luke Suen/Shutterstock.com; p. 35 (bottom) Vudhikrai/Shutterstock.com; p. 37 (top) Laura Dinraths/Shutterstock.com; p. 37 (bottom) Aqua Images/Shutterstock.com; p. 40 Tim Laman/National Geographic/Getty Images; p. 42 Wang LiQiang/Shutterstock.com; p. 44 De Agostini Picture Library/Getty Images.

Contents

Introduction

Whether it was for Halloween, a school play, a comic book convention, or just for fun, most people have worn costumes and pretended that they were someone else. Maybe they dressed up as someone they admired, such as a TV or movie star, or perhaps a super hero. Or maybe they were trying to look like someone that would frighten anyone that saw them.

In nature, some animals have ways of pretending to be something they are not. But they are not just doing this for fun. They are mimicking, or pretending to be a different creature, to survive.

Creatures that mimic other animals are usually not dangerous. In fact, they are often defenseless.

But because they can mimic creatures their predators fear or do not want to eat, they have a big advantage. Animals that might otherwise want to eat them are likely to leave them alone.

There are many ways for animals to appear to be something they are not. Some stay safe from predators by blending in with their surroundings. This is called **camouflage**. Examples of this are insects that look like a stick or a leaf. Their ability to camouflage makes it hard for predators to see them. When a bird or other creature looking for a quick lunch passes by, they probably won't notice the camouflaged insects are there. As a result, the insects are much less likely to be eaten.

Some creatures have other ways of fooling predators. They can stay safe without having to blend in with their surroundings. They do not use camouflage at all. In fact, they often stand out because their skin or their wings are so brightly colored. But still, predators do not bother them. Hungry animals avoid these mimics not because of what they are, but because of what they look like. In the animal kingdom, bright colors often mean that an animal is poisonous. And unless food is very scarce, most predators will not take a chance on eating an animal that might make them sick or kill them.

But avoiding predators is not the only benefit animals can gain from mimicking. Some animals mimic the appearance or behavior of other creatures as a way to get a meal. This type of mimicking is called

The anglerfish's lure glows in the darkness of the deep sea. The glow comes from bacteria. Only females have the lures.

Introduction

aggressive **mimicry**. Sometimes, these animals go as far as pretending to be a creature its prey would want to eat. One example of this kind of mimicry is the anglerfish. This prehistoric-looking fish lives near the bottom of the ocean. It has a bony "fishing rod," called a lure, growing above its head that it uses to attract its prey. The lure looks like a worm to a hungry fish. When the fish swims over to investigate, it becomes the anglerfish's meal. An anglerfish's mouth is so big, it can swallow prey up to twice its own size!

The term "mimic" comes from the Greek word "mimetikos," which means imitation. The word was originally used to describe people that imitated others. But in the mid-1800s, scientists began to use the word "mimic" to describe any creature that has the ability to imitate.

Chapter 1

Imitators Are Everywhere!

Most people have heard the expression, "Don't be a copycat!" But in the wild, being a copycat can save an animal's life. Camouflage and mimicry are two ways for animals to be copycats. Sometimes, it can be hard to tell camouflage and mimicry apart. For example, animals with bodies that look like leaves or sticks use camouflage, not mimicry. These animals do look like something else, but they are using their shape and color to hide. True mimics do not hide at all. They can usually be seen very easily. But they look like something predators want to avoid!

Sometimes mimics are brightly colored, like poisonous animals. These colors warn other animals to stay away. There are other mimics that have the shape of more dangerous animals, such as snakes, ants, or wasps. It can be hard to tell the difference between a mimic and a truly dangerous animal. So predators usually leave both the dangerous animals and the look-alikes alone.

Bad-Tasting Butterflies

There are two main kinds of mimics. They are called Batesian and Mullerian. Each kind is named after the scientist who discovered it. In the 1800s, British scientist Henry Bates (1825–1892) took a trip to the Amazon jungle in South America. Bates gathered different kinds of butterflies. He noticed that there were many butterfly species that looked very similar. Bates had to study them closely to make sure he put them in the right group.

He learned that some of the butterflies were bad-tasting. Animals knew not to eat them. There were also butterfly mimics that looked like the bad-tasting ones. They, too, were left alone by other animals. In this kind of mimicry, an animal that is usually safe to eat looks like one that is not safe.

Years later, a German scientist named Dr. Fritz Muller (1821–1897) discovered that Bates was only partly right. Dr. Muller found that mimics were not always harmless. Sometimes even the mimic was dangerous. In this type of mimicry, two dangerous animals looked the same. So neither is eaten more often than the other.

In order for mimicry to work well, a few things have to happen. First, both the mimic and the animal it copies must live in the same area. Otherwise, predators would have no reason to fear it or not want to eat it.

An ant-mimicking jumping spider lifts its two front legs to look like antennae.

Next, it helps if the mimic animal also acts like the animal it is copying. For example, there are many kinds of spiders that mimic ants. By lifting two of their eight legs, they look like six-legged ants. Most ants taste bad or can give a nasty sting, so many animals (with a few exceptions, such as anteaters) do not try to eat them.

Heads or Tails?

Some animals use a defense called **self-mimicry** to keep predators away. In self-mimicry, one part of the animal's body looks like another. For example, many types of caterpillar have tail-ends that look exactly like

Dangerous Colors

Bright colors serve different functions in the wild. They can help an animal attract a mate. Mostly, however, warning colors—usually red, orange, or yellow—tell others to stay clear! Some animals with colorful bodies are poisonous. Others are bad-tasting or stinky. One taste of the brightly colored animals and predators quickly learn to avoid them.

their heads. Predators almost always attack the head of their prey, which is a good way to kill it. If the predator accidentally attacks the tail end of a self-mimicking caterpillar, that caterpillar has a chance to get away.

Other mimics use fake "eyes" called **eyespots** to avoid being eaten by predators. An owl butterfly, for example, has one large dark spot on each bottom wing. With the wings fully opened, it looks like the face of

A foureye butterflyfish has a large dark spot surrounded by a white ring on either side of its tail.

Fun Fact!

The foureye butterflyfish is named for the eyespots on its tail.

an owl. This can confuse a predator looking for a snack. Another example is a type of Brazilian frog that has two big, dark spots on its rear. When it is scared, it puffs up its body and sticks its bottom up in the air. It looks like a bigger animal that's not afraid to face its attacker.

Moreover, if the eyespots are far enough from the animal's head, the predator may be fooled into attacking the eyespot area instead. The mimic might have a chance to escape with just a nibble on its tail or wing.

Chapter 2

Copycat Snakes

Some snakes that are not **venomous** look very much like those that have a deadly bite. For example, the harmless king snake looks very much like the dangerous coral snake. The coral snake has red bands next to yellow bands. Certain kinds of king snakes have red bands next to black bands. The patterns are similar enough to keep predators away. This is an example of Batesian mimicry, which is a harmless animal mimicking a dangerous one.

People that live in regions where these snakes can be found have come up with catchy rhymes to help them remember which snakes to avoid, such as "Red on yellow kills a fellow. Red on black is a friend of Jack."

The nonvenomous Sierra Mountain king snake (*top*) looks too much like the deadly coral snake (*bottom*) for predators to risk attacking it.

Some king snakes are also able to mimic the body shape of a coral snake. Most snakes have heads that are wider than their bodies, but coral snakes have very slim heads that are the exact same size as their bodies. The Mexican milk snake is one type of king snake that can mimic the body shape of a coral snake.

Colors That Say Stay Away!

With its red, yellow, and black bands and its body shape, the Mexican milk snake is one of the best coral snake mimics. This clever mimic is found mostly in the southern parts of Texas and parts of Mexico. Mexican milk snakes share that area with the Texas coral snake.

Both snakes are really shy. Even though the Texas coral snake moves around during the day, it stays hidden. The Mexican milk snake hides also. Both snakes usually stay under piles of leaves or among logs or tree stumps. But with their bright warning colors, they would be safe even without hiding. Most predators know to stay away even if the snakes are out in the open. After the sun goes down, these snakes come out in search of food.

Fun Fact!

King snakes can eat rattlesnakes, copperheads, and coral snakes without getting sick.

When Mimicking Doesn't Help

The coral snake has very few enemies. Its mimic, the king snake, can actually squeeze a coral snake to death and eat it. But hawks and other large birds are the coral snake's biggest threats. Other animals have learned to stay away from the deadly coral snakes and their mimics.

Unfortunately, the same colors that protect king snakes can also harm them. Since they look so much like coral snakes, people often kill them. People see the bright colors and panic. They kill the snake before checking to see if it might be a mimic or not.

Caterpillars That Mimic Snakes

Snakes are not the only animals that can mimic other snakes. Some of the best snake mimics are much tinier than any snake. They are caterpillars. Many caterpillars will raise the front of their bodies up in the air when threatened. To many other animals, this looks like a snake.

Acting Tough

Looking like a dangerous animal is one trick a harmless critter may use to survive. Acting like one is another trick. For example, the harmless bull snake will often imitate a deadly rattlesnake by hissing, coiling up, and shaking its tail if bothered. These traits are enough to make most predators keep their distance. But if these behaviors don't work, the bull snake will actually strike at a predator! Bull snakes are constrictors, which means they squeeze their food to death. In other words, they have no venom and are not dangerous. Still, a bite from a bull snake could be very painful.

An elephant hawk moth caterpillar's front end can puff up to resemble a snake's head, keeping predators away.

One of the most amazing of these mimics is the hawk moth caterpillar. It has a big black spot on each side of its head. These eyespots look like scary snake eyes. If that is not enough to frighten off predators, the caterpillar will move its body back and forth like a snake. At that point, very few predators would risk coming close enough to eat it!

Chapter 3

Bad-Tasting Bugs

Monarch butterflies have bright orange and black markings. These warning colors make them beautiful to look at, but dangerous to eat. They taste bad and can make birds that mistake them for lunch very sick.

The viceroy butterfly has the same colors as the monarch. This helps protect it from birds that have learned that monarchs are bad to eat. For many years, scientists thought the viceroy was not harmful to birds. Now, they have learned that the viceroy is bad-tasting, and can also make birds sick. Both butterflies are harmful to birds, and both are protected by looking alike. This is an example of Mullerian mimicry.

Monarch butterflies (*top*) and viceroy butterflies (*bottom*) look almost identical. But the viceroy has a line going across the bottom of its wings.

Eating Toxic Plants Give Protection

Monarch and viceroy butterflies may look the same, but their caterpillars do not. The monarch caterpillar has black, yellow, and white bands. The viceroy caterpillar is brown with white splotches, making it resemble bird droppings. This is a form of mimicry, too. The viceroy caterpillar looks like something gross that no animal would want to eat.

The food monarchs and viceroys eat as caterpillars is what makes them poisonous. The monarch caterpillar only eats the milkweed plant, which is toxic. The viceroy caterpillar eats willow leaves, which are also toxic. Both kinds of caterpillars will still have these poisons in their bodies after they become butterflies.

Once the caterpillars have eaten and grown, they each form a **chrysalis**. The monarch's chrysalis is large, smooth, and bright green. The viceroy's chrysalis is bumpy and brown. But when the monarch and viceroy butterflies finally come out of their chrysalises, they look almost exactly alike. The only way to tell a viceroy from a monarch butterfly is a thin line. The viceroy has a black line across both of its back wings. The monarch does not. The viceroy is also a little smaller than the monarch. But these subtle differences are not enough to help birds tell the two apart.

Looking Like Someone They Know

Viceroy butterflies live all over the United States. Some even live in southern Canada and in Mexico. Monarch butterflies are found in only some of these places. Mimicry works only if the mimic looks like another animal in its area. If there are no monarchs around, it does not help the viceroy to look like one.

That Looks Like Poop!

For most animals, poop is not a delicious treat. Therefore, looking like poop would help an animal avoid being eaten. The caterpillar of the giant swallowtail butterfly, for example, is dark with white patches and has lumpy, bumpy body coverings. It mimics bird droppings!

For example, viceroy butterflies in Florida are not bright orange and black like monarchs. They are a deeper brown and black like the queen butterfly, a close cousin of the monarch. There are far more queen butterflies in Florida than orange monarchs, so in Florida, it is better for a viceroy butterfly to look like a queen butterfly rather than a monarch butterfly.

A Mouthful of Pain

Butterflies are not the only bugs that mimic. Some flies and moths mimic the colors and body shapes of bees or

Fun Fact!

The big, bright monarch butterfly is named that because it is considered to be the king of butterflies!

A hoverfly's wasp-like yellow and black coloring, body shape, and hovering protect it from becoming another animal's lunch.

wasps. Few animals eat bees or wasps because of their painful sting.

These mimics also act like wasps and bees by eating the same types of flower nectar or fruits or making a buzzing sound. They also copy the way a wasp or bee flies by hovering in the air and quickly darting here and there.

Chapter 4

Amphibian Clones

When predators see a red **eft**, another name for a young red spotted newt, they know not to bother it. It has bright orange or red skin with several spots on its back. Just about any animal that eats a red eft would be killed by its poison. The red salamander mimics the red eft's color.

Both the red eft and the red salamander live in the same areas. Salamanders and newts are **amphibians**. This means that they can live both in water and on land. They also go through a few different stages of life before becoming adults. They begin their lives in the water as eggs. After the eggs hatch, they look very similar to frog tadpoles. (Newts and salamanders do not lose their tails like tadpoles do, however.)

The red eft (*top*) and its mimic, the red salamander (*bottom*), are both poisonous. Predators avoid both of them.

As they grow, the baby newts and salamanders lose their **gills**, which help them breathe underwater. Next, they grow legs and lungs, which allow them to breathe on land. By now they have their bright red spotted skin.

Out and About

Red efts and red salamanders spend their time resting under rocks or logs, but they do not need to hide from other animals. Their bright red, poisonous skin protects them by warning predators to stay away. So predators usually leave both amphibians alone. Looking alike helps both the red eft and the red salamander stay safer. Neither the red eft or its mimic has a greater chance of being nibbled than the other.

Spotting the Difference

The dark spots on the back of the red eft and red salamander are the best way to tell the two animals apart. The red eft has black rings around dark red spots. The red salamander's spots are black.

Fun Fact!

Salamanders have the amazing ability to regrow limbs, tails, and even parts of their organs!

Both amphibians have poisonous skin, but the red salamander's toxin only stings and burns the unlucky animals that try to eat it. However, the red eft's poison can kill an animal very quickly. Like almost all salamanders and newts, the poisons are made naturally by the red eft's body. It does not get its poison from the food it eats.

Only Deadly for a While

After two or three years, the eft turns into an adult red-spotted newt. Its skin changes from bright, spotted red to a dull, olive green. Then it moves back to water to live. Now it is also much less poisonous than it was as an eft.

The red salamander's copycat act works only when there are red efts living nearby. If there were no deadly red efts around, predators might learn in time that the red salamander was not as dangerous. Maybe its bad taste would be worth it for a hungry predator. But luckily for the red salamander, new red efts are always coming on land to grow into red-spotted newts. And as long as there are red efts, predators are not likely to take a chance. So, the red salamander stays safe.

Poisonous Jungle Frogs

Some of the most poisonous animals in the world are the beautifully colored poison dart frogs. They are most

The Imitators

Different species of imitator salamanders each look like another kind of salamander. Most imitator salamanders look like Jordan's salamanders. The Jordan's salamander has a black body and bright red legs and cheeks. It is very poisonous. The imitator salamander has the same black body and bright red cheeks, but it is not toxic.

Amphibian Clones

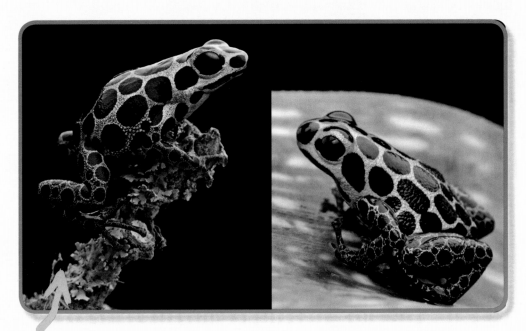

The Zimmerman's poison dart frog (*left*) and the imitator poison dart frog (*right*) are both toxic and left alone by other animals.

often found in rain forests. Their bright rainbow colors warn other animals of the toxins in their skin.

The imitator poison dart frog is a tiny frog found in the jungles of Peru. It has bright green or yellow skin with large black dots all over its body, just like the Zimmerman's poison dart frog, which also lives in Peru. Since they look like each other, neither of them has a greater chance than the other of being eaten.

Chapter 5

Marine Masters of Deception

When it comes to mimicking, the mimic octopus takes the prize. It can mimic so many things that a predator would hardly know where to start looking for it. Not only can it change color to match its surroundings, but it can also mimic the behavior of other ocean animals, such as a stingray, jellyfish, lionfish, starfish, or snake.

The mimic octopus can grow up to 24 inches (61 centimeters) long. It is usually brown-and-white striped. Its body shape is the same as any other octopus. All octopuses are **cephalopods**. They have a large, sac-like body, which floats behind their heads. An octopus has two large eyes on top of its head. Behind those eyes is one of the smartest brains of any ocean animal.

Fun Fact!

Before 1998, no human had ever seen the mimic octopus. Then divers discovered it on the bottom of a muddy river mouth in Indonesia.

Hiding and Hunting

Scientists have found that the mimic octopus usually spends most of the day sitting still in its sandy burrow waiting for small shellfish and other fish to pass by.

Sometimes the mimic octopus slowly crawls along the estuary floor. When it is on the hunt, the mimic octopus looks like any other octopus. It is not trying to hide or disguise itself. But when frightened or bothered, it changes its shape to look like dangerous ocean animals.

Sometimes the mimic octopus flattens itself out. It puts all of its arms close to its body. When swimming like this, it looks just like one of the poisonous brown-and-white striped sole fish found in the area. Predators would most likely avoid these types of fish, so they also avoid the mimic octopus.

Other times, the mimic octopus swims with all eight arms spread wide to look like the deadly lionfish, which is also brown and white striped. It has large, poison-filled spines along its back and sides.

Scientists have also seen a female mimic octopus floating on top of the water with all her legs hanging down. They think she may have been imitating a jellyfish, which are famous for their painful stings!

Pretending to Be a Snake

Scientists have also seen the mimic octopus act like a sea snake several times to keep damselfish away. The small but aggressive damselfish will attack anything that comes near its home, including a mimic octopus.

A mimic octopus (*top*) spreads its arms to resemble the dangerous lionfish (*bottom*).

One animal the damselfish is afraid of, however, is the sea snake. The damselfish can be part of a sea snake's diet. Whenever the mimic octopus is bothered by damselfish, it mimics the sea snake. The octopus puts six legs down in the sand. It lets two legs float free. This looks very much like the striped sea snakes that live in the same area.

The mimic octopus seems to decide what poisonous animal to mimic. It changes its look to fit the situation. It is one smart mimic!

Flatworm or Fish?

Some flatworms taste bad, while others are toxic. Many are brightly colored as a warning to stay away. Therefore, many species of fish try to look like flatworms to avoid being eaten. The pinnate batfish mimics the flatworm's bright colors and the unique way it swims. The flatworm moves through the water in a wavelike, fluttering motion. The pinnate batfish will go on its side and wave its fins in a similar way.

The comet (*top*) mimics the white-mouth moray eel (*bottom*) to scare off predators.

Fooled by Fish

Some fish are mimics also. The mostly vegetarian pacu looks like its meat-eating cousin, the piranha. Both fish are found in the Amazon River in South America. The pacu is a good mimic of the feared piranha . . . unless you look in its mouth! Piranhas have pointy, sharp teeth to strip the flesh from its prey. Pacu teeth look very much like human teeth! And that's because, like humans, pacu eat meat and plants. They use their teeth to crush the fruit and plants that fall from the trees.

The white-mouth moray eel is another famous, fearsome creature of the deep. It has a brown snakelike body with white spots and two lines of sharp teeth that help it hold onto its prey. Eels are usually seen with just their heads sticking out of their caves. The comet is a fish with the same coloring and an eyespot on its top fin. When the comet is threatened, it will hide in a hole with only it's tail sticking out. To other animals, this looks like a moray eel, not dinner!

Chapter 6

Bird and Mammal Mimics

There are very few mammal or bird mimics. The main reason is that for mimicry to exist, one of the animals has to be poisonous or bad-tasting. There are no poisonous mammals or birds, right? Wrong! There actually are a few types of birds that are poisonous.

The hooded pitohui (PIT-oo-wee) is one of these. It lives in New Guinea. This bird has poisonous feathers and skin. Scientists believe this bird gets its poison from beetles that it eats.

The hooded pitohui has a black body. It has bright red and yellow feathers around its neck and shoulders. These bright feathers tell other animals that the bird is

The hooded pitohui's poison is the same type found in some poison dart frogs.

poisonous. A few other kinds of birds in New Guinea have the same colored feathers as the hooded pitohui. This makes predators think they are poisonous, too.

Mimicking to Make Life Easier

Some birds use mimicry to make their lives easier. The fork-tailed drongo, a type of bird that lives in Africa, uses mimicry as a trick to help it steal food. When a fork-tailed drongo sees meerkats eating something that looks tasty, it sometimes mimics the sound of a meerkat's "alarm call" to scare them away. An alarm call is the sound an animal makes if it sees a predator coming. Sometimes the meerkats quickly figure out they have been tricked and return to the food. But some fork-tailed drongos have a plan B. They can also mimic the sound of predators that eat meerkats to keep them away.

Another bird that uses mimicry to make its life easier is the cuckoo. Cuckoos live in parts of Europe, Asia, and Africa. But cuckoos do not mimic to avoid predators or obtain food. Instead, they mimic to make other birds hatch their eggs and raise their young!

When a female cuckoo is ready to lay her eggs, she does not build a nest of her own. Instead, she searches for the nest of another bird. When the mother bird is away from the nest searching for food, the cuckoo pushes at least one of the original eggs out of the nest. She then lays one of her own. The cuckoo egg is often slightly larger and a different color than the

A reed warbler feeds a cuckoo chick. The chick is bigger than the mother bird, but the warbler doesn't seem to notice it's not her own baby.

original eggs. But when the mother bird returns, she usually doesn't notice that one of her eggs has been replaced.

Often, the cuckoo chick hatches before the other eggs. It pushes the others out, so it is the only chick left. It gets all the food the parent birds bring. Even after it grows too big for the nest, the parents will continue to feed it. Meanwhile, the cuckoo's real mother has been leaving eggs in other birds' nests for them to hatch and raise.

Fun Fact!

Scientists call animals that trick other species into raising their young obligate brood parasites. This kind of mimicry can be found among birds, insects, and fish.

When Humans Mimic

Throughout history, humans have also found ways to hide in plain sight. They camouflage or mimic. When humans go hunting, they often wear clothes that are the same colors as the trees. This makes it difficult for animals they are hunting to see them. This is called camouflage clothing. Some soldiers also wear camouflage clothing so their enemies cannot see them.

Double Trouble

The maned rat, also called a crested rat, is a large rodent that lives in Africa. Scientists think it mimics two different species. It has long hair along its back that it can raise when it is scared. The raised hairs resemble the sharp quills of a porcupine. No predator wants a face full of quills! The maned rat may also mimic a zorilla, an animal in the weasel family that looks like and sprays like a skunk. The black-and-white coloring of the maned rat mimics that of the zorilla. Most animals wouldn't risk being sprayed either!

This painting of a maned rat shows its similarities to the armored porcupine and smelly zorilla.

Bird and Mammal Mimics

In almost every war, spies have played an important role in helping to learn about an enemy. Spies have to know how to dress, talk, and act like the enemy. They have to learn the language of the country in which they are spying. They also have to study the ways of the people they are spying on. Many times, spies will wear disguises to look like the local people. Costumes and makeup help change their appearance. The only way to be safe is by being a perfect mimic. Any mistake could mean disaster, just like in the animal world.

Mimics and Their Many Tricks

In the animal world, mimics are masters of deception. While some animals use camouflage to hide, mimics take their tricks even further. Their defense is to look scarier, yuckier, or bigger than they really are. Mimics might look like something dangerous. They might look like something disgusting. They may even be dangerous or disgusting themselves! However they look, their copycat ways keep them safe and able to hide in plain sight.

Glossary

amphibian A cold-blooded animal, such as a frog or salamander, that can live both on land and in water.

camouflage A defense in which an animal's coloring or shape helps it hide from predators.

cephalopod A type of animal, such as an octopus or squid, that has several long arms and a very large head.

chrysalis A hard case in which a caterpillar turns into a butterfly.

eft A young newt.

eyespot A dark, round marking on an animal's body that looks like a eye.

gills The organs of a fish or other water-dwelling animal that allows it to breathe underwater.

mimicry A defense in which an animal has the appearance of a more dangerous animal in order to fool predators.

self-mimicry A defense in which part of an animal's body looks like another part, such as a false head.

venomous Producing a substance that becomes toxic when injected into a victim, usually through biting.

warning colors Colors that let other animals know that a creature is poisonous.

Further Reading

Books

Johnson, Rebecca L. *Masters of Disguise: Amazing Animal Tricksters.* Minneapolis, MN: Lerner Publishing Group, 2016.

Kroll, Jennifer. *Showdown Animal Defenses.* Huntington Beach, CA: Teacher Created Materials, 2017.

Light, Kate. *Why Do Some Moths Mimic Wasps? And Other Odd Insect Adaptations.* New York, NY: Gareth Stevens Publishing, 2018.

Lindeen, Mary. *Animal Defenses.* Chicago, IL: Norwood House Press, 2018.

Websites

Explorable: Camouflage and Mimicry
explorable.com/camouflage-and-mimicry
Learn more about camouflage and mimicry.

Field and Swamp: Mimicry, Camouflage, and More
www.dpughphoto.com/mimicry.htm
Read more about animals that mimic other animals.

OctopusWorlds: Mimic Octopus
www.octopusworlds.com/mimic-octopus/
Discover more interesting facts about the mimic octopus.

Index